Messages of

TRUST

for Lent 2020

D0685726

Messages of

TRUST

for **Lent 2020**

3-MINUTE DEVOTIONS

MICHAEL WHITE and **TOM CORCORAN**

Ave Maria Press AVE Notre Dame, Indiana

© 2019 by Michael White and Tom Corcoran

Founded in 1865, Ave Maria Press is a ministry of the United States Province of Holy Cross.

www.avemariapress.com

Paperback: ISBN-13 978-1-59471-941-7

E-book: ISBN-13 978-1-59471-942-4

Cover and text design by Samantha Watson.

Printed and bound in the United States of America.

Introduction

Fulton Sheen once said about our first pope, Peter, "He hated discipline. In other words, he was like everybody else." We all know we need to grow in discipline, and we know we don't want to. Lent is a discipline, and most of us would have to admit we don't really like it. We'd also have to admit we need it. Lent invites us into a season of greater spiritual discipline that includes prayer, penance, and almsgiving. This discipline, in turn, pushes us outside our comfort zone and challenges our usual orientation in life.

We all have a mental framework in which we understand God, a paradigm or conception of how things work from which we interpret the world and life around us. This is absolutely necessary for us if we are to maintain our balance and organize our lives and relationships. However, at times we need the gift of disorientation. This is because in times of disorientation we are confronted with fresh facts or new truths that cannot be ignored and do not fit within our old ways of comprehending the world.

Jesus brought the gift of disorientation into first-century Palestine. He did this over and over again with just about every group and individual with whom he interacted. He brought disorientation to the religious leaders of the time. They could not understand how Jesus could both fulfill the Law and at the same time receive and dine with sinners. He brought disorientation to sinners and outcasts. They were shocked to learn that they could have access to the kingdom of heaven, that God would welcome them as sons and daughters. And Jesus constantly disoriented his closest friends and followers on just about everything from religious rule keeping to the measure of true greatness.

Lenten discipline introduces disorientation into our ordinary lives, and that's why it's so important for our continued growth in discipleship. As you work your way through these brief scripture passages and messages about growing in trust, we pray that you will experience the gift of disorientation. We pray that your heart will be touched and your mind will be stretched to grow.

In turn may you receive another gift—the gift of reorientation. This occurs when we synthesize new insights and understandings with our old paradigms. We learn that our old understanding was not wrong, just limited. Our minds and hearts are expanded to receive more of the blessings and grace of God.

May your Lenten journey bring you to a new and deeper understanding of God your Father and a more expansive trust in the ways of the Lord. May Lent bring you greater appreciation for the joy and the triumph of Christ's resurrection. Through this season of grace may you come to know more fully the fruits of the Holy Spirit, who leads you always toward the glory of heaven.

Fr. Michael and Tom

WEEK OF
Ash Wednesday

Wednesday, February 26

Yet even now—oracle of the LORD—return to me with your whole heart, with fasting, weeping, and mourning. Rend your hearts, not your garments, and return to the LORD, your God, For he is gracious and merciful, slow to anger, abounding in steadfast love, and relenting in punishment. Perhaps he will again relent and leave behind a blessing,

—Joel 2:12–14

The prophet Joel is speaking to a people who are suffering greatly. Their survival depends on agriculture, so when they suffer a great locust infestation that brings the destruction of their crops, the people are deeply distressed. But things get even worse for the Israelites as a powerful enemy from the north threatens to destroy them.

The situation is bad, yet the people feel they can't turn to God because they have rejected him for so long. Joel assuages those fears, assuring them that God is merciful.

God is gracious and slow to anger, but we never know for certain what God is going to do. Perhaps God will relent, perhaps not. But we do know with certainty his character. Our task is to fast and pray, to give and serve. Our task is to trust in the Lord, even when his actions don't make sense to us.

....

Pray that during this Lent you will return to the Lord with your whole heart and grow in greater trust of God's character, especially his mercy and kindness to you.

Thursday, February 27

Gather the people, sanctify the congregation;
Assemble the elderly; gather the children, even
infants nursing at the breast; Let the bridegroom
leave his room and the bride her bridal tent.
—Joel 2:16

Through the prophet Joel, the Lord tells the people to repent and turn back to him, even if only as an act of desperation. While every person must choose to repent, it is meant to be a communal act: including the nursing children to the elderly. So urgent is the need for repentance that even couples preparing to marry should stop what they are doing and join in the fasting and prayer.

....

Ask God to show you today how your Lenten journey can be taken with others. Perhaps God is encouraging you to gather your family for prayer on a daily or weekly basis. Perhaps it means going to daily Mass and connecting with the people there. Ask God to show you how he wants you to grow with others this Lent.

Friday, February 28

Then the LORD grew jealous for his land and took pity on his people.

—Joel 2:18

The Israelites are facing a catastrophe because they have no food and an enemy is threatening them. They know they have ignored God, yet through the prophet Joel, the Lord encourages his people to fast and pray. Joel says it is not too late to seek the Lord, and he tells them to not just go through the outward motions of repentance and spiritual renewal but to truly change their hearts. He tells them to gather together as a community in prayer and to trust in God's mercy.

The second chapter of Joel tells us that God took pity on his people as a result of their communal fasting and prayer. He sent grain, new wine, and oil to satisfy their need for food. He protected them from the enemy to their north. Their fasting and prayer made a difference.

Prayer and fasting change outcomes. They invite God's mercy and intervention. It is a mystery we will never fully understand, but it is a truth repeated in scripture over and over again.

....

Pray today for the grace to believe that your prayer and fasting make a difference in your life and in the world.

Saturday, February 29

Psalm 86

Teach me your way, O Lord, that I may walk in your truth.

Incline your ear, O LORD; answer me,
> for I am afflicted and poor.

Keep my life, for I am devoted to you;
> save your servant who trusts in you.
> You are my God.

Teach me your way, O Lord, that I may walk in your truth.

Have mercy on me, O LORD,
> for to you I call all the day.

Gladden the soul of your servant,
> for to you, O LORD, I lift up my soul.

Teach me your way, O Lord, that I may walk in your truth.

For you, O LORD, are good and forgiving,
> abounding in kindness to all who call upon
> > you.

Hearken, O LORD, to my prayer
> and attend to the sound of my pleading.

Teach me your way, O Lord, that I may walk in your truth.

First Week

OF LENT

Sunday, March 1

As we move into the first full week of Lent, responding to the call to turn back to the Lord with prayer and fasting, we examine times when God appears to say no to things that seem good. On these occasions, it can sometimes seem that God wills or wants a bad thing for us or is not powerful enough to make what we want happen. What is our response to this? How do we turn and trust the Lord?

This first week of Lent, we will be looking at this mystery through the second creation story, of Adam and Eve and the tree of the knowledge of good and evil. There we will see how even when God says no, there is a much richer yes yet to be revealed.

....

Today, ask for the grace to be more open to receiving and responding to God's will in your life in a positive and life-giving way.

Monday, March 2

The LORD God planted a garden in Eden, in the east, and placed there the man whom he had formed. Out of the ground the LORD God made grow every tree that was delightful to look at and good for food, with the tree of life in the middle of the garden and the tree of the knowledge of good and evil.

—Genesis 2:8–9

Genesis tells us that when God created the world, all was perfect. There was harmony with creation, between the first humans, within themselves, and with God. As part of this order, every living creation always acted in accordance with God's will.

When God had the world as he wanted, there was only one rule for the first humans: do not eat from the tree of the knowledge of good and evil. Every other tree could be enjoyed. God did not want to keep good things from human beings but wanted them to enjoy his creation.

....

Thank God today that he is a good God who invites you to enjoy his creation.

Tuesday, March 3

Now the snake was the most cunning of all the wild animals that the LORD God had made. He asked the woman, "Did God really say, 'You shall not eat from any of the trees in the garden'?"

—Genesis 3:1

God said Adam and Eve could not eat from only one tree, but the snake twists these words. He makes God sound very controlling, as if he doesn't want Eve to enjoy life. The snake places a seed of doubt in Eve's mind, which eventually leads to the Fall of humanity.

We are tempted in the same way today. We are tempted to see God as giving us a bunch of rules that limit our freedom. We are tempted to distrust God's goodness so that we see his laws and teachings as impediments to a good life and not the path of life.

....

Ask God today for the grace to remember that he doesn't give his laws and teachings to keep us from the good life but rather to lead us to the good life.

Wednesday, March 4

The woman answered the snake: "We may eat of the fruit of the trees in the garden; it is only about the fruit of the tree in the middle of the garden that God said, 'You shall not eat it or even touch it, or else you will die.'" But the snake said to the woman: "You certainly will not die! God knows well that when you eat of it your eyes will be opened and you will be like gods, who know good and evil."

—Genesis 3:2–5

The snake tells Eve: God is holding out on you. God is keeping good things from you. God doesn't want you to eat the fruit because he wants to control you. God is against you and not for you. If you want to have a great life, you need to get rid of God and go on without him. Your life would be so much better without God. He is not the cause of happiness but an obstacle to it.

This is what the Evil One does. He works to steal our trust in God, so that we question God's intentions and love for us. Good parents know that they must protect their children from evil in the world, evil their kids don't even understand. A parent saying no to something that may bring harm to a child is a sign of love deeper than children can comprehend from their limited life experience.

....

Where do you hear God saying no this Lent? Ask God for greater faith to recognize his yes in your life. Ask the Lord to teach you to trust.

Thursday, March 5

The woman saw that the tree was good for food and pleasing to the eyes, and the tree was desirable for gaining wisdom. So she took some of its fruit and ate it; and she also gave some to her husband, who was with her, and he ate it.

—Genesis 3:6

Everything God created was good. God did not create evil. Evil entered the world because God gave humans free will—the ability to choose good or evil—and humans chose to misuse God's good creation for harmful ends. The serpent's lie is not saying the fruit is good or attractive. The lie is that this particular good thing, this piece of fruit, is meant for Eve to eat.

This deception happens often in life. We see things that look good on the surface, that seem desirable, but God knows they are not good for us. So he tells us they are off limits. Like Eve, we will be tempted to eat the fruit, to make a decision that will cause us harm in the end.

....

Pray for the grace today to recognize and refuse the forbidden fruits that will bring unnecessary pain to your life.

Friday, March 6

> Then the eyes of both of them were opened, and they knew that they were naked; so they sewed fig leaves together and made loincloths for themselves.
>
> —Genesis 3:7

Suddenly, their eyes were opened and their lives changed forever. But it was a life God had not intended: one with sin and death, lacking peace and perfect harmony. Instead of satisfaction, Adam and Eve felt ashamed.

God wanted to protect humanity from the pain and shame that came from eating the forbidden fruit. He told them no, so they would not experience evil. God says no to protect us from evil. He is not keeping something from us but is for us.

....

Today, ask God to help you accept every no and yes on your daily faith journey. Pray that you learn to trust God, even when his answer seems tough or painful.

Saturday, March 7

Psalm 119

Blessed are they who follow the law of the Lord!

Blessed are they whose way is blameless,
 who walk in the law of the LORD.
Blessed are they who observe his decrees,
 who seek him with all their heart.

Blessed are they who follow the law of the Lord!

You have commanded that your precepts
 be diligently kept.
Oh, that I might be firm in the ways
 of keeping your statutes!

Blessed are they who follow the law of the Lord!

I will give you thanks with an upright heart,
 when I have learned your just ordinances.
I will keep your statutes;
 do not utterly forsake me.

Blessed are they who follow the law of the Lord!

Second Week

OF LENT

Sunday, March 8

This week we will look at our human experience with suffering and death. We struggle with how, when, and why suffering and death occur in our lives—this may be the hardest question we ever have to confront. While we will never make full sense of it, this week's reflection on the Transfiguration helps us understand that a future glory awaits every experience of suffering and death.

....

As the second week of Lent begins, meditate on the Cross, the point where our suffering intersects with Christ's sacrificial love.

Monday, March 9

After six days Jesus took Peter, James, and John his brother, and led them up a high mountain by themselves. And he was transfigured before them; his face shone like the sun and his clothes became white as light. And behold, Moses and Elijah appeared to them, conversing with him.
—Matthew 17:1–3

The radiant appearance of Jesus in Matthew's telling of the Transfiguration reveals the divinity of the Christ, showing that he is both fully God and fully human. The appearance of Moses and Elijah reinforces that Jesus is the fulfillment of God's promise to save his people.

That Jesus is both fully divine and fully human means his story will include glory and honor as well as suffering and death. As we grow as disciples of Jesus, we learn to see our own stories—our accomplishments, successes, failures, sufferings, and death—in the light of that story.

Today, pray for those in your life who are experiencing suffering or the effects of losing a loved one. Pray that they find the strength to trust the Lord's ways.

Tuesday, March 10

Then Peter said to Jesus in reply, "Lord, it is good that we are here. If you wish, I will make three tents here, one for you, one for Moses, and one for Elijah."

—Matthew 17:4

Peter sees the glory of Jesus, and he is awestruck. It is so good that he wants to stay there, and he tries to get Jesus to stay. Surely, he thinks, *Why can't following Jesus always be like this? Why go any further?*

It is good when we have these mountaintop experiences in our faith, but like a photograph, they only capture a moment and not the whole story. To stay on the mountaintop would be a temptation to Jesus to avoid his mission and escape the horror of the Cross that awaits him.

....

Today, ask God to equip you with the grace of trust you will need to face with courage and patience whatever suffering or tragedy comes your way in life.

Wednesday, March 11

While he was still speaking, behold, a bright cloud cast a shadow over them, then from the cloud came a voice that said, "This is my beloved Son, with whom I am well pleased; listen to him."

—Matthew 17:5

In this middle of Peter's request to set up camp on the mountain, God the Father interrupts him. Matthew records here the same words spoken at the Baptism of Jesus in the Jordan River (3:17): "This is my beloved Son, with whom I am well pleased; listen to him."

God does not stop loving Jesus, even though he allows his beloved Son to undergo suffering and death. It does not please the Father to see his children suffer. There is no greater mystery and tragedy, nothing that seems to make less sense than the death of someone we love, especially if the time and circumstances seem random or wrong. God does not give us any easy answers. Instead, he gives us his Son, to be with us always, especially in times of suffering and death.

....

Today, spend some quiet time, away from distractions, to "listen to him" as the Father tells us to do.

Thursday, March 12

When the disciples heard this, they fell prostrate and were very much afraid. But Jesus came and touched them, saying, "Rise, and do not be afraid." And when the disciples raised their eyes, they saw no one else but Jesus alone.

—Matthew 17:6–8

The Old Testament taught that people could not look upon the face of God and live, so the disciples fall prostrate to hide themselves. Jesus tells them not to be afraid, and when they look up, only he remains.

Sometimes, our desire for answers from God comes from a need to be in control of our circumstances. When we don't feel in control, we feel afraid. But this assumes we would be less afraid if we knew the answers to questions such as, "Why suffering and death?" or that any answer would suffice. The peace of Jesus goes deeper than the kind of mental satisfaction we feel when we have the answers to our questions. Jesus accepts our questions and still says to us, "Do not be afraid."

....

Tell God what things make you feel afraid. Ask God to stay near to you in your questions where you don't feel like you have a good answer.

Friday, March 13

As they were coming down from the mountain, Jesus charged them, "Do not tell the vision to anyone until the Son of Man has been raised from the dead." Then the disciples asked him, "Why do the scribes say that Elijah must come first?" He said in reply, "Elijah will indeed come and restore all things; but I tell you that Elijah has already come, and they did not recognize him but did to him whatever they pleased. So also will the Son of Man suffer at their hands."

—Matthew 17:9–12

Because they have not yet witnessed the Resurrection, the disciples are susceptible to drawing the wrong conclusions about Jesus and his mission.

Jesus does not bring about a kingdom of political power but rather a kingdom that restores life and creation to be as God intended. Death and suffering were not part of God's creation; they entered the world through sin. The Transfiguration points to a restoration and ultimate redemption of all persons and things, what our Christian faith calls "salvation." God is at work now in our world, but God's kingdom is not yet complete. Jesus conquered death, and we can confidently trust that death will not have the final word.

....

Today, pray that God will restore the broken and suffering people of the world. Ask for the healing of relationships you see in your communities and in the media—if not in this life, then in the life to come.

Psalm 103

The Lord is kind and merciful.

Bless the LORD, O my soul;
 and all my being, bless his holy name.
Bless the LORD, O my soul,
 and forget not all his benefits.

The Lord is kind and merciful.

He pardons all your iniquities,
 he heals all your ills.
He redeems your life from destruction,
 he crowns you with kindness and compassion.

The Lord is kind and merciful.

He will not always chide,
 nor does he keep his wrath forever.
Not according to our sins does he deal with us,
 nor does he requite us according to our crimes.

The Lord is kind and merciful.

THIRD WEEK
OF LENT

Sunday, March 15

On the surface, it's not difficult to come up with our own lists of things that God does or doesn't do, says or doesn't say, that do not make sense to us. This week we will be looking at times when God appears to put obstacles in our way, things we think prevent us from making progress or having a more successful life. Instead of viewing these as ways God discourages us, the Bible often reveals these as ways in which God tests and strengthens our faith.

....

Today, thank God for the times in your life when a difficult trial made you stronger in faith by teaching you to better trust the Lord. Pray for patience and courage in hard times that may lay ahead.

Monday, March 16

From the wilderness of Sin the whole Israelite community journeyed by stages, as the LORD directed,
and encamped at Rephidim. But there was no
water for the people to drink, and so they quarreled with Moses and said, "Give us water to drink."
—Exodus 17:1–2

Having led his people out of slavery in Egypt, God
pledged to lead the Israelites to the Promised Land,
a land flowing with milk and honey. But at this
point in their journey, they are stuck in the wilderness with not enough to eat or drink. They turn
on their leader, Moses, and start to blame him for
their situation. Rather than being patient or asking
how they can help, they become demanding. Their
hearts are hardening against God and against his
servant.

When we face obstacles and difficulties, we
have a choice—do we grumble and complain, or
do we trust God to provide for our needs?

....

Name some of the things you often grumble and complain about. Pray for the grace to turn to God rather
than grumble and complain about them.

Tuesday, March 17

Moses replied to them, "Why do you quarrel with me? Why do you put the Lord to a test?" Here, then, in their thirst for water, the people grumbled against Moses, saying, "Why then did you bring us up out of Egypt? To have us die of thirst with our children and our livestock?"

—Exodus 17:2–3

Out in the wilderness, God tested the Israelites to see if they were as committed to their covenant as he was. It was a test they had failed before, and he was giving them another chance to pass. Rather than passing the test, they actually tested God as if he needed to prove himself to them. They forgot who they were and in confusion tried to judge God instead of acknowledging God as ultimate judge.

Hard times and difficulties test us. And through these trials, God gives us the opportunity to strengthen and improve ourselves, to choose to grow into people who trust him no matter the circumstances.

....

Ask God to help you see the challenges you are facing not as hindrances to block your path to joy and success but as tests to improve and strengthen your faith for the future.

Wednesday, March 18

So Moses cried out to the LORD, "What shall I do with this people? A little more and they will stone me!" The LORD answered Moses: Go on ahead of the people, and take along with you some of the elders of Israel, holding in your hand, as you go, the staff with which you struck the Nile. I will be standing there in front of you on the rock in Horeb. Strike the rock, and the water will flow from it for the people to drink. Moses did this, in the sight of the elders of Israel. The place was named Massah and Meribah, because the Israelites quarreled there and tested the LORD, saying, "Is the LORD in our midst or not?"

—Exodus 17:4–7

God never appears to someone in the Bible and says, "I have a really easy job for you, and even the small obstacles I will smooth out so that you don't notice them." Nothing worth accomplishing is ever easy, but these obstacles are opportunities to lean into God. If we are willing to lean into God and depend on his grace, we will see his power as Moses did.

But if we choose to grumble and complain, we will miss out on his power. God's power works through human weakness when we choose to trust him. He wants us to learn to rely upon him and his grace so we can become who he created us to be.

Ask God for the gift of humility to learn the lessons you need to be able to pass the tests of faith that will come your way today.

Thursday, March 19

Therefore, that I might not become too elated, a thorn in the flesh was given to me, an angel of Satan, to beat me, to keep me from being too elated. Three times I begged the Lord about this, that it might leave me, but he said to me, "My grace is sufficient for you, for power is made perfect in weakness." I will rather boast most gladly of my weaknesses, in order that the power of Christ may dwell with me.

—2 Corinthians 12:7–9

Paul writes that he had a thorn in his flesh to keep him from becoming too elated or too conceited. God allowed the wound to keep Paul humble, and while Paul begged God to remove this "thorn," God did not so that Paul would come to rely upon grace.

God allows thorns in our lives too so that we will learn to rely upon his power and grace. When we rely on God's grace completely, we see his power and might, which far exceeds our abilities to handle difficult situations on our own.

....

Where does God want you to lean into his grace and power? Ask God to help you to see your problems as an opportunity to receive his power.

Friday, March 20

> Not only that, but we even boast of our afflictions, knowing that affliction produces endurance, and endurance, proven character, and proven character, hope, and hope does not disappoint, because the love of God has been poured out into our hearts through the holy Spirit that has been given to us.
> —Romans 5:3–5

Paul makes an argument why the afflictions we face, if looked at in the right way, all work to produce greater good and hope in our lives. We know that a community that faces pain and obstacles together grow into a community that hopes together. When we begin to see the obstacles that stand in our way as opportunities for the Lord to strengthen us in faith, we can develop the kind of endurance and character that will be able to withstand whatever comes our way.

....

Today, ask God for the strength to endure whatever afflictions you are going through so that you can grow in the character of his Son, Jesus.

Saturday, March 21

Psalm 40

Here I am, Lord; I come to do your will.

Sacrifice or oblation you wished not,
  but ears open to obedience you gave me.
Holocausts or sin-offerings you sought not;
  then said I, "Behold I come."

Here I am, Lord; I come to do your will.

"In the written scroll it is prescribed for me,
To do your will, O my God, is my delight,
  and your law is within my heart!"

Here I am, Lord; I come to do your will.

I announced your justice in the vast assembly;
  I did not restrain my lips, as you, O LORD,
    know.

Here I am, Lord; I come to do your will.

Fourth Week

OF LENT

Sunday, March 22

This week, we will dig into how injustice and corruption seem to have an edge over humble and godly leadership. When we see things we don't like in politics, in our workplaces, in our schools, and—perhaps most painfully—in our Church, we may wonder why God would allow bad leaders to determine the direction of our communities and lives.

In Jesus, we find a leader who is constantly available to those who are mistreated or who suffer injustice. He reveals that God allows injustice and that by experiencing the weakness of earthly kingdoms, we can be changed deep in our souls and compelled to work for the kingdom of God.

....

Today, pray for the people who lead our Church, our country, and our communities, that they may lead well even when we disagree with their decisions and actions.

Monday, March 23

As Jesus passed by he saw a man blind from birth. His disciples asked him, "Rabbi, who sinned, this man or his parents, that he was born blind?" Jesus answered, "Neither he nor his parents sinned; it is so that the works of God might be made visible through him. We have to do the works of the one who sent me while it is day. Night is coming when no one can work. While I am in the world, I am the light of the world." When he had said this, he spat on the ground and made clay with the saliva, and smeared the clay on his eyes, and said to him, "Go wash in the Pool of Siloam" (which means Sent). So he went and washed, and came back able to see.

—John 9:1–7

In this gospel story, Jesus dispels two unjust ideas in the religious culture of his day. First, while people assumed that an illness and disability were the result of one's own or one's parents' wrongdoing, Jesus assures his disciples that God loves these people equally, and they become special witnesses of his love. Second, Jesus works his healing miracle on the Sabbath, a day when work wasn't permitted.

In both cases, Jesus wants to help those near him identify the priorities of his Father. Through this story Jesus teaches us to see others not with the lens of judgment but with eyes of love and mercy so we may know that the God of healing and love is accessible to all people, at all times, in all places.

....

Ask God today to help you see and notice in a new and loving manner those people you tend to overlook or avoid.

Tuesday, March 24

They brought the one who was once blind to the Pharisees. Now Jesus had made clay and opened his eyes on a Sabbath. So then the Pharisees also asked him how he was able to see. He said to them, "He put clay on my eyes, and I washed, and now I can see." So some of the Pharisees said, "This man is not from God, because he does not keep the Sabbath." But others said, "How can a sinful man do such signs?" And there was a division among them.

—John 9:13–16

According to the religious law of the day, Jesus was breaking the law by healing on the Sabbath. But Jesus exposed the corrupt and unjust hearts of many of the Pharisees by this action. These Jewish leaders were threatened by him. In their spiritual blindness, the Pharisees turn the very thing that reveals Jesus is of God into evidence against him.

This is what we often see in corrupt authority—the use of power not to serve others but to safeguard personal interests. We see this in our workplaces, schools, community organizations, and also in ourselves when we seek to control outcomes that benefit us more than others. But Jesus heals our vision when we learn to serve others before tending to our own greedy interests.

....

Today, look for an opportunity to lower yourself and lift up someone else—by taking the seat in the back or a parking space far from the door or by deflecting praise from yourself toward someone else who is deserving.

Wednesday, March 25

The man answered and said to them, "This is what is so amazing, that you do not know where he is from, yet he opened my eyes. We know that God does not listen to sinners, but if one is devout and does his will, he listens to him. It is unheard of that anyone ever opened the eyes of a person born blind. If this man were not from God, he would not be able to do anything." They answered and said to him, "You were born totally in sin, and are you trying to teach us?" Then they threw him out.

—John 9:30–34

The religious leaders were supposed to be able to identify the true messiah when he came. But because they had become more concerned about protecting the rules than having a relationship with God, they were unable to see the Messiah when he was standing right in front of them. That is the truly amazing thing the formerly blind man understands.

The Pharisees refuse even to listen to what the blind man has to say. Their corrupt hearts lead to corrupt vision: they only see things one way and refuse to consider any other possibility, resulting in a spiritual myopia. When other people and events challenge our beliefs, remember that only the Lord can open our eyes to the truth of sin and redemption.

....

Today, take time to have a conversation and listen to someone with whom you wouldn't normally relate. Ask God to lead that person into closer relationship with himself.

Thursday, March 26

> When Jesus heard that they had thrown him out, he found him and said, "Do you believe in the Son of Man?" He answered and said, "Who is he, sir, that I may believe in him?" Jesus said to him, "You have seen him and the one speaking with you is he." He said, "I do believe, Lord," and he worshiped him. Then Jesus said, "I came into this world for judgment, so that those who do not see might see, and those who do see might become blind."
>
> —John 9:35–39

The blind man, although treated unjustly by the religious authorities, develops a personal relationship with Christ. Even though God allows imperfect and unjust people to wield earthly authority, Jesus reveals the heavenly meaning of power, as he makes himself available to all, especially those who are mistreated or suffer injustice.

God allows injustice because experiencing the weakness of this earthly kingdom often drives us to his heavenly kingdom. No matter what injustice you or your loved ones have experienced because of the misuse of earthly authority, Jesus stands ready to comfort you and reveal himself to you more completely.

....

Today, pray for those who are your "enemies," people who have caused you stress or aggravation.

Friday, March 27

Some of the Pharisees who were with him heard this and said to him, "Surely we are not also blind, are we?" Jesus said to them, "If you were blind, you would have no sin; but now you are saying, 'We see,' so your sin remains."

—John 9:40–41

The Pharisees are surprised to consider that they themselves might have sin in their hearts because they have been so scrupulous in following the religious laws of the day. So, too, we should not assume that our hearts are pure. Rather, we should make a habit of evaluating our own thoughts and actions before God in prayer so that we do not develop self-righteous or self-aggrandizing habits.

....

Today, spend time examining your conscience, letting Jesus come into your heart and revealing the ways you still need to see your sin and his mercy.

Saturday, March 28

Psalm 7

O Lord, my God, in you I take refuge.

O LORD, my God, in you I take refuge;
    save me from all my pursuers and rescue me,
Lest I become like the lion's prey,
    to be torn to pieces, with no one to rescue me.

O Lord, my God, in you I take refuge.

Do me justice, O LORD, because I am just,
    and because of the innocence that is mine.
Let the malice of the wicked come to an end,
    but sustain the just,
    O searcher of heart and soul, O just God.

O Lord, my God, in you I take refuge.

A shield before me is God,
    who saves the upright of heart;
A just judge is God,
    a God who punishes day by day.

O Lord, my God, in you I take refuge.

Fifth Week

OF LENT

Sunday, March 29

During this fifth week of Lent we will contemplate the mystery of God's timing. We've all experienced the often frustrating reality that God's timing isn't always our timing. In fact, at times it can seem that God's time is *never* what we'd like it to be. We often become frustrated that God doesn't step in and act when *we* think he ought to do so.

In this Sunday's gospel reading, Jesus goes to his friends Mary and Martha, who are mourning the death of their brother Lazarus. The women wonder why Jesus didn't come sooner, since they believe that he could have prevented the death of Lazarus. While they think Jesus is too late to do anything, his timing works a much greater miracle than they ever expected.

....

Today, ask God for the patience to accept the events and circumstances of life in God's time, not yours.

Monday, March 30

Now a man was ill, Lazarus from Bethany, the village of Mary and her sister Martha. Mary was the one who had anointed the Lord with perfumed oil and dried his feet with her hair; it was her brother Lazarus who was ill. So the sisters sent word to him, saying, "Master, the one you love is ill." When Jesus heard this he said, "This illness is not to end in death, but is for the glory of God, that the Son of God may be glorified through it."

—John 11:1–4

In this passage from John's gospel, Jesus gets news that his dear friend, Lazarus, the brother of Martha and Mary, is ill and near death. Jesus knows that what unfolds next will not end with the death of his friend but rather will greatly bless Lazarus, Martha, and Mary and bring glory to God. However, it seems that only Jesus sees this.

When we experience illness or suffer in another way, we cannot see the whole picture, but God does. His sovereignty and ability to bring good from evil is beyond our capacity to understand, yet we can be confident that God acts on our behalf always and in all things. Through his saving power God will be glorified, and more people will come to know him.

....

Today, pray to trust God in times of pain and suffering. Pray to trust in God's timing.

Tuesday, March 31

Now Jesus loved Martha and her sister and Lazarus. So when he heard that Lazarus was ill, Jesus remained for two days in the place where he was. Then after this he said to his disciples, "Let us go back to Judea."

—John 11:5–7

On the surface, the passage is confusing. Jesus hears that his beloved friend Lazarus is ill, but rather than going to him immediately, Jesus waits for two days. Most of us, if we received the news that a dear friend is near death, would head right to their side if at all possible to offer comfort and support. But Jesus, who is supposed to be better at loving than we are, doesn't rush to Lazarus but stays in place.

When our prayers aren't answered quickly, we can think God doesn't care about our needs. You may be waiting for God to answer your prayer for a job, for money, for a child, or for any number of other things. Trust that God will move in his time and not in yours.

....

Today, pray for the grace to trust in God when nothing seems to be improving with your most pressing problems.

Wednesday, April 1

When Jesus arrived, he found that Lazarus had already been in the tomb for four days. Now Bethany was near Jerusalem, only about two miles away. And many of the Jews had come to Martha and Mary to comfort them about their brother. When Martha heard that Jesus was coming, she went to meet him, but Mary sat at home. Martha said to Jesus, "Lord, if you had been here, my brother would not have died."

—John 11:17–21

By the time Jesus arrives at the home of his friends, Lazarus has died. His sisters mourn and many of the Jewish people nearby have come to comfort them. Martha goes out to meet Jesus, but Mary does not. Perhaps she is too disappointed, or maybe she is angry or simply too confused. Martha, on the other hand, shares what's on her heart: Jesus could have kept her brother from dying. Why did he wait?

When we experience pain and suffering, Martha's thought is often our thought: *God could have prevented this. If God is all powerful, he could have done something.* This perception is both true and untrue. God works in our lives but often in ways we are not looking for. God cannot both bless us with free will *and* always take the hard parts of life away. We must trust in God's judgment and timing.

....

. Are you mad or disappointed with God for not intervening in some particularly difficult circumstance of your life or the life of someone you love? Follow Martha's example, and confess this to him.

Thursday, April 2

So Jesus, perturbed again, came to the tomb. It was a cave, and a stone lay across it. Jesus said, "Take away the stone." Martha, the dead man's sister, said to him, "Lord, by now there will be a stench; he has been dead for four days." Jesus said to her, "Did I not tell you that if you believe you will see the glory of God?"

—John 11:38–40

Mary and Martha must have been confused, hurt, and likely angry that Jesus didn't come sooner to save Lazarus. Why was he avoiding the fact that Lazarus had died? Jesus wants to present a new reality, one in which he will raise Lazarus from the dead, with the help of other people. Jesus could have done all the work himself, but he didn't. Instead, Jesus told his followers to "take away the stone" because he wants each of us to take an active part in his ministry.

The Lord of the universe can work miracles through our cooperation. After we make way for God by removing the barriers, the obstacles, the stones, then God can get to work. As these barriers are removed, we are more prepared to believe in and see the glory of God.

....

Is there an area of your life where you could use a miracle? Where do you need God's intervention? Place this before God. Ask the Holy Spirit to help you see and remove even the smallest barrier so that God can act on your behalf.

Friday, April 3

So they took away the stone. And Jesus raised his eyes and said, "Father, I thank you for hearing me. I know that you always hear me; but because of the crowd here I have said this, that they may believe that you sent me." And when he had said this, he cried out in a loud voice, "Lazarus, come out!" The dead man came out, tied hand and foot with burial bands, and his face was wrapped in a cloth. So Jesus said to them, "Untie him and let him go."
—John 11:41–44

Once the stone is rolled away, Jesus gets to work. First, he thanks God the Father. Jesus attributes every success to his ever-loving, ever-listening Father. While God has heard his plea, his act of raising Lazarus back to earthly life confirms the even greater truth that God will one day raise to eternal life all who believe and trust in him.

Every disciple is called to share with others the new life they have received by believing in Jesus—not because they could die tomorrow but because we want to offer them new life in Christ.

....

Spend time in prayer today thanking and praising God for a recent success or accomplishment, and acknowledging your dependence on his power and timing.

Saturday, April 4

Psalm 18

In my distress I called upon the Lord, and he heard my voice.

I love you, O Lord, my strength,
   O Lord, my rock, my fortress, my deliverer.

In my distress I called upon the Lord, and he heard my voice.

My God, my rock of refuge,
   my shield, the horn of my salvation, my
      stronghold!
Praised be the Lord, I exclaim,
   and I am safe from my enemies.

In my distress I called upon the Lord, and he heard my voice.

The breakers of death surged round about me,
   the destroying floods overwhelmed me;
The cords of the nether world enmeshed me,
   the snares of death overtook me.

In my distress I called upon the Lord, and he heard my voice.

HOLY WEEK

Sunday, April 5

When they drew near Jerusalem and came to Bethphage on the Mount of Olives, Jesus sent two disciples, saying to them, "Go into the village opposite you, and immediately you will find an ass tethered, and a colt with her. Untie them and bring them here to me. And if anyone should say anything to you, reply, 'The master has need of them.' Then he will send them at once." . . . The very large crowd spread their cloaks on the road, while others cut branches from the trees and strewed them on the road. The crowds preceding him and those following kept crying out and saying: "Hosanna to the Son of David; blessed is he who comes in the name of the Lord; hosanna in the highest."

And when he entered Jerusalem the whole city was shaken and asked, "Who is this?" And the crowds replied, "This is Jesus the prophet, from Nazareth in Galilee."

—Matthew 21:1–3, 8–11

Jesus' entry into Jerusalem begins Holy Week, the days leading up to our commemoration of his Passion, Death, and Resurrection. Jesus enters the city with throngs of supporters, but he will die with only a few by his side. Most will deny him, betray him, walk away from him, or call for his crucifixion because he does not come to overthrow the political power of Rome, as they expected of the Messiah. But those who stay with him are richly rewarded, for they witness the Resurrection.

....

Pray as the crowd chanted: "Hosanna, to the Son of David; blessed is he who comes in the name of the Lord; hosanna in the highest." Invite Jesus into your heart to save you from sin and death.

Monday, April 6

Now when Jesus was in Bethany in the house of Simon the leper, a woman came up to him with an alabaster jar of costly perfumed oil, and poured it on his head while he was reclining at table. When the disciples saw this, they were indignant and said, "Why this waste? It could have been sold for much, and the money given to the poor."

Since Jesus knew this, he said to them, "Why do you make trouble for the woman? She has done a good thing for me. The poor you will always have with you; but you will not always have me. In pouring this perfumed oil upon my body, she did it to prepare me for burial. Amen, I say to you, wherever this gospel is proclaimed in the whole world, what she has done will be spoken of, in memory of her."

—Matthew 26:6–13

In this passage, Jesus allows an unnamed woman to anoint him with oil, which was traditionally done for priests, prophets, and kings, as well as the dead before burial. Jesus accepts this anointing because he is our priest, prophet, and king, who gave up his life to save us.

The Chrism Mass is celebrated in Catholic cathedrals throughout the world this week. During that celebration the holy oils used in Baptism, Confirmation, Holy Orders, and the Anointing of the Sick are blessed. Through these and all sacraments we participate in the identity and ministry of Jesus as priest, prophet, and king

....

Today, pray for all who lead and minister to others in the name of Christ, that they may find joy and strength to persevere in the face of challenges.

Tuesday, April 7

Jesus entered the temple area and drove out all those engaged in selling and buying there. He overturned the tables of the money changers and the seats of those who were selling doves. And he said to them, "It is written: 'My house shall be a house of prayer,' but you are making it a den of thieves."

—Matthew 21:12–13

In the days leading up to his crucifixion, Jesus openly taught in Jerusalem, which led to confrontations with the religious authorities. For Jewish people the Temple was sacred, where God himself dwelt. It was meant to be a place for prayer and religious offerings, but instead it became a place for religious leaders to control people and steal from them in the name of God. Jesus boldly and publicly denounces this abuse of authority, as he drives out the money changers from the Temple.

Through Baptism, each of us have become the place where God dwells, so we are in a sense new temples. Corruption in our hearts and souls not only hurts us but also defiles a sacred dwelling of the Lord.

....

Today, ask the Holy Spirit to clear away the dishonesty and hypocrisy in your own heart. Trust that a place for Christ to dwell will be prepared within you.

Wednesday, April 8

On the first day of the Feast of Unleavened Bread, the disciples approached Jesus and said, "Where do you want us to prepare for you to eat the Passover?" He said, "Go into the city to a certain man and tell him, 'The teacher says, "My appointed time draws near; in your house I shall celebrate the Passover with my disciples."'" The disciples then did as Jesus had ordered, and prepared the Passover.

—Matthew 26:17–19

Every year, the Jews celebrate the Passover as a memorial of Moses leading the Israelites out of Egyptian slavery. As a faithful Jew, Jesus celebrates the Passover, but he has another intention as well. He is also preparing himself for sacrifice. Through his Passion and Death, Jesus becomes the Lamb of God, who frees all people from the captivity of sin.

Jesus provides himself as the sacrifice for our sins. Like the disciples, we have preparation to do, making our hearts and souls ready to receive him.

....

Today, ask the Spirit to show you what you can do today to prepare for Jesus' Passover and sacrifice on the Cross.

Thursday, April 9

While they were eating, Jesus took bread, said the blessing, broke it, and giving it to his disciples said, "Take and eat; this is my body." Then he took a cup, gave thanks, and gave it to them, saying, "Drink from it, all of you, for this is my blood of the covenant, which will be shed on behalf of many for the forgiveness of sins. I tell you, from now on I shall not drink this fruit of the vine until the day when I drink it with you new in the kingdom of my Father." Then, after singing a hymn, they went out to the Mount of Olives.

—Matthew 26:26–30

Jesus and his disciples celebrated the Passover on Thursday evening of what we now know as *Holy Week*. At this meal, Jesus washed their feet and then instituted the Eucharist by sharing with them bread and wine, saying "this is my body" and "this is my blood." He unites service and sacrament, both of which are key to our ongoing conversion to become disciples, take up our crosses, and follow Jesus.

....

Today, give thanks for the gift of the Eucharist. Ask Jesus to lead you toward a deeper experience of his love when you receive him in the sacrament and in serving others.

Friday, April 10

From noon onward, darkness came over the whole land until three in the afternoon. And about three o'clock Jesus cried out in a loud voice, "*Eli, Eli lema sabachtani?*" which means, "My god, my God, why have you forsaken me?" . . . Then Jesus cried out again in a loud voice, and gave up his spirit. And behold the veil of the sanctuary was torn in two from top to bottom.

—Matthew 27:45–46, 50–51

After a conspiracy between the Jewish leaders and Roman authorities, Jesus is condemned to death by crucifixion. This makes no sense to his followers; they thought that the Messiah was going to free them from Roman occupation as well as corrupt Jewish leadership. Instead, Jesus dies a shameful death, looking like a complete failure. He seems to be abandoned by God and cries out, asking God why this is so. It looks like Jesus lost.

But immediately after Jesus' death, we see the first sign that all is not what it appears. The veil of the sanctuary, a very thick curtain about forty feet high, is torn from top to bottom—with no natural explanation. So too, the love of Christ, as he willfully chooses death to defeat sin for us, demonstrates the extraordinary power of God.

Thank God today for Jesus' death on the Cross, which destroyed sin and death and freed us to regain full access to our heavenly Father.

Saturday, April 11

Psalm 130

If you O Lord, mark iniquities, who can stand?
Out of the depths I cry to you, LORD;
    LORD, hear my voice!
May your ears be attentive
    to my voice in supplication.
If you O Lord, mark iniquities, who can stand?
If you, O LORD, mark iniquities,
    LORD, who can stand?
But with you is forgiveness,
    that you may be revered.
If you O Lord, mark iniquities, who can stand?
I trust in the LORD,
    my soul trusts in his word.
My soul waits for the LORD
    more than sentinels for dawn.
    Let Israel wait for the LORD.
If you O Lord, mark iniquities, who can stand?

Rev. Michael White is a priest of the Archdiocese of Baltimore and pastor of Church of the Nativity in Timonium, Maryland. He earned his bachelor's degree from Loyola University Maryland and his graduate degrees in sacred theology and ecclesiology from the Pontifical Gregorian University in Rome.

During White's tenure as pastor at Church of the Nativity, the parish has almost tripled its weekend attendance. More important, commitment to the mission of the Church has grown, evidenced by the significant increase of giving and service in ministry, and much evidence of genuine spiritual renewal. White is the coauthor of *Rebuilt*—which narrates the story of Nativity's rebirth—*Tools for Rebuilding, Rebuilding Your Message*, and *The Rebuilt Field Guide*.

Tom Corcoran has served Church of the Nativity in Timonium, Maryland, in a variety of roles that give him a unique perspective on parish ministry and leadership. First hired as a youth minister, Corcoran has also served as coordinator of children's ministry and director of small groups. He is lay associate to the pastor and is responsible for weekend message development, strategic planning, and staff development.

Corcoran is the coauthor of *Rebuilt*—which narrates the story of Nativity's rebirth—*Tools for Rebuilding, Rebuilding Your Message*, and *The Rebuilt Field Guide*.

churchnativity.com
rebuiltparish.com
rebuiltparish.podbean.com
Facebook: churchnativity
Twitter: @churchnativity
Instagram: @churchnativity